CIRCLE OF FIFTHS

EXPLAINED

BY DAN MASKE

ISBN 978-1-5400-6948-1

Copyright © 2020 by HAL LEONARD LLC
International Copyright Secured   All Rights Reserved

Visit Hal Leonard Online at
www.halleonard.com

World headquarters, contact:
Hal Leonard
7777 West Bluemound Road
Milwaukee, WI 53213
Email: info@halleonard.com

In Europe, contact:
Hal Leonard Europe Limited
42 Wigmore Street
Marylebone, London, W1U 2RN
Email: info@halleonardeurope.com

In Australia, contact:
Hal Leonard Australia Pty. Ltd.
4 Lentara Court
Cheltenham, Victoria, 3192 Australia
Email: info@halleonard.com.au

INTRODUCTION

In many music theory textbooks, the *circle of 5ths* exists as one small part of a chapter on keys and key signatures, and then again in a discussion on modulation (changing keys). However, the circle of 5ths is more than just a small topic, rather it is a major force governing how music is organized, and how the whole system and its many facets relate to each other.

To fully comprehend the circle of 5ths, one needs a basic understanding of musical concepts such as intervals, scales, keys/key signatures, and chords. However, the relationship of these concepts to the circle of 5ths is symbiotic. This means that once you start to understand the circle of 5ths, you will be able to better comprehend these other musical concepts. In other words, they help each other.

The circle of 5ths demonstrates how keys relate to each other. In this book, after chapters dealing with intervals and scales to help set the stage, the chapter on key signatures will fully explain exactly what the circle of 5ths is and how it is constructed. This explanation will then set up the circle of 5ths to be used as a tool in dealing with chords and chord progressions in the context of actual music.

Before delving into these topics, a brief definition of the circle of 5ths may be useful. It is a graphic image of all keys arranged in a circle. Since there are twelve different pitches in the chromatic scale, the circle resembles the face of a clock. A clock, with hands which move around and around in a circle, has no real beginning nor end. The same is true of keys, and so this clock analogy may be helpful in understanding and memorizing these relationships and the circle of 5ths itself. And the "5th" in "circle of 5ths" refers to the interval between adjacent keys on the circle. Intervals will be fully explained later in the book.

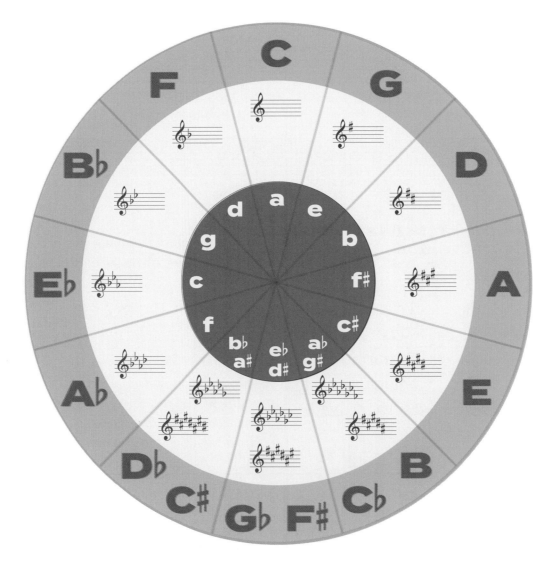

CHAPTER 1: INTERVALS

Intervals measure musical distance. While this book deals specifically with the interval of the 5th, a famil-iarity with all intervals will help to set the stage for a demonstration as to why the 5th is perhaps the most important interval in music. Besides, intervals are an important component in scales and chords, both of which are part of the backbone of music, and both have a special relationship to the circle of 5ths. A com-plete understanding of all intervals will help in using the circle of 5ths in a number of practical ways.

An interval is the distance between two pitches. There are two elements used in determining a complete identification of an interval: *interval size* and *interval quality*. In addition, each interval has a counterpart of sorts, known as its *inversion*.

INTERVAL SIZE

When attempting to identify an interval, the first step is to determine the *interval size* (sometimes referred to as *arithmetic distance*). This is done by counting the letter names of the two pitches of which we are measuring the distance, plus the letter names in between. For example, when considering A up to B, "A" is one and "B" is two, thus this distance is a 2nd. Similarly, A up to C would be a 3rd ("A" is one, "B" is two, and "C" is three: 3rd).

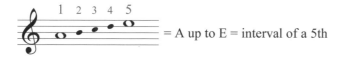 = A up to B = interval of a 2nd

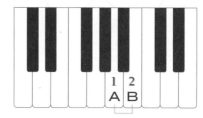

= A up to C = interval of a 3rd

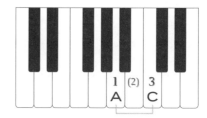

= A up to E = interval of a 5th

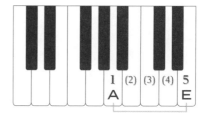

You can continue counting up the alphabet like this, all the way until reaching the 8th, more commonly referred to as the *octave*. Labeling the distance beyond the octave, one can use "9th," 10th," etc., or "octave plus 2nd, octave plus 3rd," etc.

INTERVAL QUALITY

To further and more completely identify an interval, one must determine the *interval quality*. An A up to C is a 3rd, but what type of 3rd is it? If you refer to the piano keyboard, you'll notice that in counting the white keys, A up to C, you reach a 3rd. But considering both white and black keys, this 3rd encompasses three half steps (from A up to B♭ is one, B♭ up to B is two, and B up to C is three). If we consider C up to E, also a 3rd, this distance encompasses four half steps. Both intervals are 3rds, but we must have a way to differentiate between these two types of 3rds, as they are in fact different distances. Thus, we have different interval qualities, such as *perfect, major, minor, diminished*, and *augmented*.

Perfect

The intervals of the *unison*, 4th, 5th, and octave are the only four intervals which may be labeled "perfect." Long ago, in the Medieval and Renaissance periods, these were the only intervals considered appropriate for places of rest or resolution, such as the ending of phrases. Thus, the label "perfect" was used to describe these intervals.

To figure out these "perfect" intervals, one might count the number of half steps, use the major scale, or both (in cases of uncertainty, where you wish to check your work, it may be beneficial to use both methods). For example, a perfect 5th consists of seven half steps. G is seven half steps above C, thus a perfect 5th. However, it is important to make sure to have the correct interval size, in other words, the correct letter names. B up to F♯ is seven half steps, but so is B up to G♭. But B to G♭ is not a 5th, rather it is a 6th.

An octave is perhaps the simplest interval to demonstrate this important detail. C♯ up to the next C♯ is an octave (a perfect octave, to be precise). But although D♭ up to C♯ involves the same two pitches as C♯ up to C♯, we cannot call this an octave, because an octave must have the same two letter names. Consider the 2nd, an interval we know to consist of two adjacent letters in the alphabet. C♯ up to D♯ is a 2nd. But C♯ up to E♭ is not, rather it is a 3rd. Spelling matters, and it matters in a variety of ways that have to do with musical context. The perfect interval of the *unison* describes two or more parts playing the same note at the same octave (e.g., two voices both singing middle C). To learn more about this musical context, further study on the subject of intervals is recommended, beyond what is necessary for the purposes of this book.

The other method which may be used to measure perfect intervals is to use the major scale (see Chapter 3 for the complete discussion of scales). In a major scale, from the 1st degree (1) to the 4th degree (4) is a perfect 4th (P4). From 1 to 5 is a perfect 5th (P5).

Major

Counting half steps and/or using the major scale may be used to measure major intervals. Using the major scale, from the 1st degree to the 2nd, 3rd, 6th, and 7th degrees of the scale, are all major intervals (2nd, 3rd, 6th, and 7th, respectively).

The following chart shows the number of half steps that each of these major intervals span.

INTERVAL	No. of HALF STEPS
Major 2nd	2
Major 3rd	4
Major 6th	9
Major 7th	11

Minor

Some musicians prefer to use major scales, major chords, and major intervals as a reference point to figure out those which pertain to minor. Having these "major" elements memorized means one can quickly get to anything minor. For example, if you know that C up to E is a major 3rd, you can lower (or shrink) the interval by a half step to turn it into a *minor interval*. But remember, you must maintain the same two letter names. So, lowering the E to E♭ gives you C up to E♭, which is a minor 3rd.

This concept will be applied later in the book to both scales and chords.

But in case you don't have the major intervals fully memorized, the following chart illustrates the number of half steps involved in each minor interval.

INTERVAL	No. of HALF STEPS
Minor 2nd	1
Minor 3rd	3
Minor 6th	8
Minor 7th	10

Diminished

Diminished intervals are one half step smaller than their minor or perfect counterparts. For example, C up to E♭ is a minor 3rd, and so C up to E♭♭ is a diminished 3rd. It's the equivalent of two half steps (or, a whole step), but since the spelling involves two letter names with one letter between them (D), it's still identified as a 3rd rather than a 2nd.

Making a perfect interval smaller by a half step produces a diminished interval. C up to G is a perfect 5th, but change the G to a G♭, and it becomes a diminished 5th.

The following chart shows all diminished intervals starting from C, including the number of half steps which span each distance.

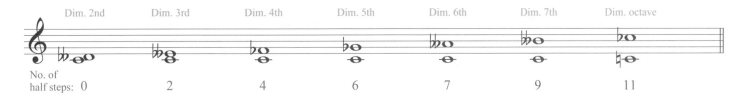

Some of the spellings may look strange to you, especially those where *double flat* symbols are used (a double flat lowers a note by two half steps). While the diminished 5th and diminished 7th are often found in music, the other diminished intervals are not commonly seen.

Augmented

Taking a major or perfect interval and increasing the distance by one half step results in an *augmented interval*. As always, remember that the letter names must remain the same. Meaning, if C up to G is a perfect 5th, then spelling an augmented 5th up from C results in a G♯ and not an A♭. C up to A♭ would be a 6th. Similarly, the major 3rd spanning C up to E becomes an augmented 3rd when the E is raised to E♯. Even though one would commonly see this distance spelled as a C up to an F (a perfect 4th), there are cases where the musical context (largely having to do with the key of the music) requires that this F be spelled as an E♯. Think of words which sound the same, but are spelled differently (i.e., "night" and "knight"). If someone were to simply say the word "night" alone, but not as part of a sentence, you wouldn't know the meaning of the word. But used in a sentence such as "The knight drew her sword, getting ready to defend herself," it becomes clear why this word needs to be spelled as "knight," even though "night" may be easier to spell. The same is true for music. For a more detailed examination on this topic of spelling notes in relation to their musical contexts, it is suggested you take on a more expansive study of music theory.

For now study the following chart, which shows augmented intervals starting on C, along with the number of half steps of which each interval consists. It is recommended you make similar charts for intervals beginning on any and all pitches (i.e., all augmented intervals up from D, etc.).

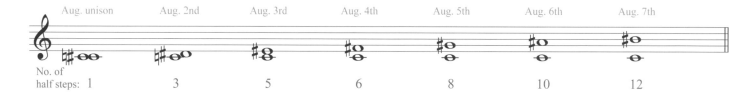

	Aug. unison	Aug. 2nd	Aug. 3rd	Aug. 4th	Aug. 5th	Aug. 6th	Aug. 7th
No. of half steps:	1	3	5	6	8	10	12

Inversions

Every interval has a counterpart called an *inversion*. Inversions are arrived at when the lower tone in an interval becomes the higher one, or vice versa. For example, C up to G is a perfect 5th, but C *down* to G is a perfect 4th. So, the 4th is an inversion of a 5th. C up to E is a 3rd, while C down to E is a 6th. And in terms of quality, the inversion of a perfect interval is another perfect interval. The inversion of a minor interval is a major interval, and the inversion of an augmented interval is a diminished interval. The following shows all inversions of intervals.

Interval	When Inverted, Interval Becomes
Perfect	Perfect
Major	Minor
Minor	Major
Diminished	Augmented
Augmented	Diminished
2nd	7th
3rd	6th
4th	5th
5th	4th
6th	3rd
7th	2nd

THE 5TH/4TH SIGNIFICANCE

The interval of the perfect 5th is what's behind the design of the circle of 5ths and the system of tonal music in general. And considering that the inversion of the perfect 5th is the perfect 4th, it will become clear why the 4th is also an important structural element in the circle of 5ths.

The remainder of this book will focus on many of the ways the interval of the 5th/4th is important in tonal music, from how the different keys are organized and their relationships with each other, to the structure of scales, to chords and chord progressions. But before this, the following serves as a brief exposure to some of the other ways the 5th/4th appears in music, including a possible origin story as to why this interval became embedded in our musical system.

Overtone Series

When we hear an instrument play a *pitch* (frequency, meaning how high or low a note sounds), what's producing the sound is vibration. The A above middle C is producing 440 vibrations (or "cycles") per second. "Cycles per second" is referred to as "hertz," often abbreviated as Hz.

But the main pitch, A440, referred to as the *fundamental*, is not the only pitch being sounded when we hear most instruments. There are other smaller/faster vibrations (called *overtones*) occurring at the same time, but with less volume. These overtones and their relative volumes to each other and the fundamental are what give the instrument its distinguishing sound. For example, a violin playing A440 sounds different than a flute playing A440, because of the differences in the overtones.

However, exactly what pitch the overtones are sounding is the same on all instruments. It's only their volumes that are different, which are in different configurations from one instrument to another. For example, when an instrument plays A440, the next overtone occurs an octave above that A. After that, the next overtone occurs at the E, an octave plus a perfect 5th above the fundamental. The next faster vibration occurs a perfect 4th above the E, in other words, two octaves above the fundamental. This keeps going, with each overtone getting closer and closer together, until we reach an overtone pitch which is three octaves above the fundamental (in actuality, overtones continue even higher than that, getting even closer together, but these pitches conform less and less to our standard tuning system). So, when you hear a violin play A440, you are also hearing all of these other higher pitches above it at the same time. But since the fundamental A is much louder than the overtones, what we perceive is just one overall pitch.

The following chart shows a complete *overtone series*, starting on a low C. The term *partials* refers to the complete set of all overtones, including the fundamental, of which there are 16. Thus, the fundamental is labeled as "partial 1."

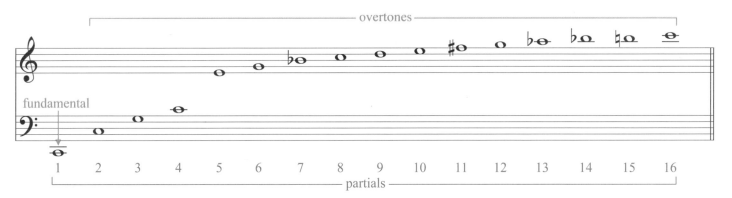

This overtone series shows an instance of an acoustical phenomenon, something which occurs naturally, where the interval of the 5th and 4th sit atop the fundamental structure of sound. After the octave, the first interval in the overtone series is a perfect 5th. And after that, we traverse the interval of a perfect 4th to arrive at the next overtone. It's no wonder our musical system of tonality holds these intervals in such high regard.

Instrument Tuning

Many instruments use the 5th/4th as a basis for how they are tuned. Or, the overtone series is the concept behind how the instrument works.

Strings

Orchestral string instruments such as violin, viola, and cello are tuned in perfect 5ths. These instruments are comprised of four strings, and beginning with the lowest pitched string, each subsequent string is a perfect 5th above the lower one. The following shows the tuning pitches of each string, beginning with the lowest.

Violin

Viola

Cello

The bass (sometimes called an "upright bass" or "double bass") shares the same tuning as an electric bass. These instruments are tuned in 4ths.

Bass

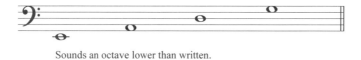

Sounds an octave lower than written.

The guitar is tuned mostly in 4ths. The interval between the G and B strings is a major 3rd. Note that this interval is also prominent in the overtone series, as it occurs between the 4th and 5th partials.

Guitar

Sounds an octave lower than written.

Brass

Have you ever wondered how a brass instrument such as a trumpet can play many different pitches over the span of multiple octaves, using only three valves? A trumpet player changes his/her *embouchure* (placement of lips and jaw in relation to the mouthpiece), as needed, to play lower and higher notes. For example, playing middle C on a trumpet requires no valves to be pushed down. If the player tightens the embouchure, the air speed changes, and without pressing in valves, a G will sound, a perfect 5th up from the C. Tighten the embouchure a bit more, and another C will sound, an octave above the original C. As the player keeps tightening the embouchure, the resulting pitches (all with the same "no valves" pressed down) go right up the overtone series: (middle) C, G, C, E, G, B♭, C.

Pushing down different combinations of valves results in a different fundamental and the subsequent pitches in the overtone series. This is how the trumpet is able to play all 12 chromatic pitches, in multiple octaves.

Woodwinds

Woodwind instruments such as the clarinet, saxophone, oboe, bassoon, and flute follow a similar principle to that of the brass instruments.

So, whether it's how the instrument is tuned, or the fact that the overtone series guides how the instrument can sound the pitches it does, the 5th/4th is something present at the most basic level. It's an interval that would seem to be a natural starting point in playing the instrument, especially at early experience levels.

SUMMARY

An understanding of the 5th interval is important in learning how the circle of 5ths is constructed. A complete understanding of all intervals will help in using the circle of 5ths in a number of practical ways. It is recommended that you study and memorize how to spell and identify intervals, not only as they appear in written music, but also how they sound. Be able to play them on your instrument, sing them, and identify them as you hear them played and sung.

CHAPTER 2: SCALES

A *scale* is a collection of pitches arranged in an ascending or descending pattern of half steps and whole steps. The vast majority of music in existence is based on some type of scale. While there are many different types of scales, which usually consist of five to eight pitches, this book will concern itself with those most common to western classical music (from before 1900) and most varieties of popular music: the major and minor scales. It's important to have a basic understanding of scales and be familiar with scale degree names, as these often get used in any discussions about music theory topics, including the subsequent chapters in this book.

THE MAJOR SCALE

The *major scale* consists of seven pitches, one for each letter of the musical alphabet. It is arranged in a particular pattern of half steps and whole steps. Beginning on C, the major scale consists of all "white keys" or all "natural" pitches (no sharps or flats).

C Major Scale

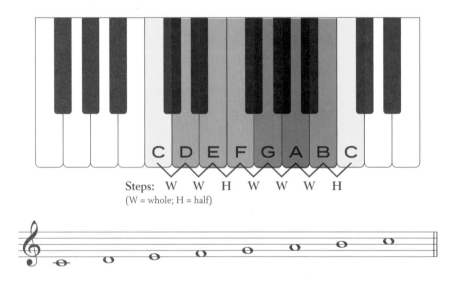

Each pitch on the scale is referred to as a *degree*. The degree is basically a number indicating where the pitch exists in the order of the notes of the scale. For example, in a C major scale, C is referred to as scale degree 1. D would be scale degree 2, and so forth. These scale degrees also have names, shown in the following table. It may be helpful to memorize these scale degree names, not only for the purposes of this book, but to better participate in musical conversation. It can be a real time saver when communicating with band mates and any other musicians with whom you might work, if everyone is speaking the same language.

Scale Degree Number	Scale Degree Name
1	Tonic
2	Supertonic
3	Mediant
4	Subdominant
5	Dominant
6	Submediant
7	Leading Tone

In tonal music, it's the relationship between the tonic and the dominant which lies at the heart of how most music works. And it's not only the pitches, but also the chords built from these two scale degrees which govern the structure of tonal music. And of course, since these two scale degrees are a 5th apart, this relationship is especially relevant to the circle of 5ths. In addition to the tonic and dominant, there are similar relationships between other scale degrees which lie a 5th apart, such as the supertonic and submediant, and any degrees separated by this interval. And because the 4th is the inversion of the 5th, there is also a special connection between scale degrees separated by this interval, as well. More on these special relationships will be discussed in "Chords and Progressions."

Besides learning the scale degree names in order, it is recommended you also learn to list them in order of 5ths and 4ths. This will help in being able to quickly recall chord relationships and better communicate ideas to other musicians. The following illustrates the scale degree names in ascending 5ths as well as 4ths, using the C major scale. To learn these in the order of 4ths, simply recite the 5ths in reverse order.

Scale Degrees in Order of 5ths and 4ths

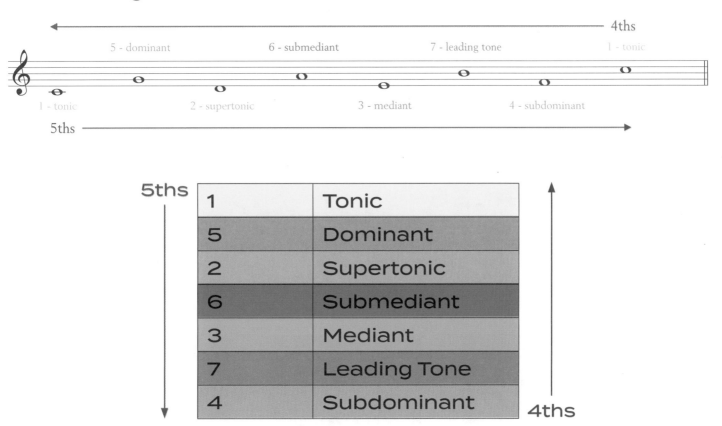

One can also use the circle of 5ths to figure out the pitches of any major scale. Using the outer circle in the following diagram, choose the pitch which corresponds to the name of the major scale you wish to compile. Next, select the first five letter names immediately clockwise of the starting pitch, plus one letter immediately counterclockwise of that pitch. Now, you have the seven pitches of that major scale, albeit out of sequence. Simply put them in alphabetical order, and you have the major scale, in ascending order. The following diagram uses E♭ as an example.

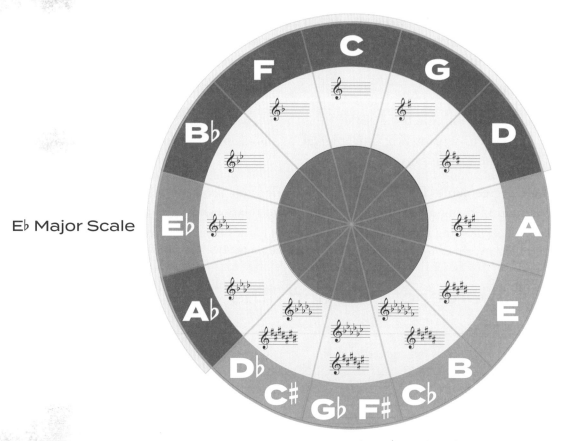

Eb Major Scale

Ascending Order: Eb, F, G, Ab, Bb, C, D

MINOR SCALES

There are three minor scales: *natural minor*, *harmonic minor*, and *melodic minor*. The natural minor scale also consists of seven pitches in a pattern of whole steps and half steps. If we begin on A, the pattern results in another scale, which consists of all white keys/natural notes.

A Natural Minor Scale

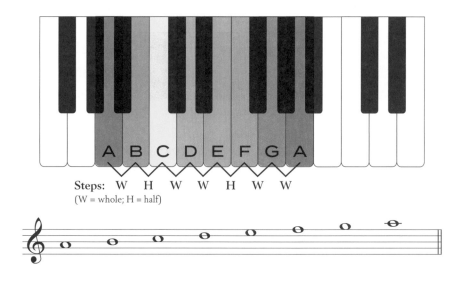

It should also be noted that, between the major scale and minor scale(s), the names for the first six scale degrees are the same. However, in the natural minor scale, where the 7th degree is a whole step beneath the tonic, we refer to this degree as the *subtonic*. (The leading tone leads, by virtue of being a half step beneath the tonic, whereas the whole step does not produce the same sense of leading.)

Another way of determining the natural minor scale is to know the major scale, then make alterations to it. Taking a major scale, lower the 3rd, 6th, and 7th degrees by one half step and you'll have the natural minor scale.

The *harmonic minor* scale consists of the same pitches as the natural minor, but raises the 7th degree a half step. So, the A harmonic minor scale would see the G raised to G♯.

A Harmonic Minor Scale

If you take the natural minor scale and raise both the 6th and 7th degrees a half step, what results is the *melodic minor* scale. However, this alteration is only employed when playing the scale in ascending order. When playing the scale in descending order, the 6th and 7th degrees are restored. So, on the way down, the natural minor and the melodic minor scales are identical.

A Melodic Minor Scale

Why are there three different minor scales? The reasons date back to music of the Classical era (1750–1820), with composers such as Haydn, Mozart, and Beethoven. It's already been mentioned that the tonic and dominant have a special relationship in tonal music. The dominant chord (the chord built from the 5th degree of the scale) wants to resolve to the tonic chord. A large part of this resolution has to do with the fact that the dominant chord is major, where the 3rd of the chord happens to be the 7th degree (leading tone) of the scale. This leading tone is a half step below the tonic, which really helps produce the demand for it to resolve, providing a certain amount of tension. This half step also makes for a satisfactory resolution, when the dominant chord progresses to the tonic chord.

In a minor key, the chord built on the 5th degree of the scale is minor. Consider the key of C minor for the following explanation, and refer to the musical examples, which help illustrate this. Based on the pitches of the natural minor scale, the dominant chord would be G minor. In music of the Classical era, if a phrase were to end on the tonic chord (Cm), it would be preceded by the dominant to give it a satisfactory kind of punctuation. To produce this satisfaction, this G minor chord would need to be turned into a major chord by raising the B♭ to B♮. Because of this need to change the harmony, a piece in C minor would see quite a few B naturals throughout. For this reason, we derive the harmonic minor scale.

Minor v resolving to tonic

Major V resolving to tonic

For reasons of melody (or *melodic motion*), we have the melodic minor scale. If a melody in C minor were to end on a C, with the notes before it stepping up to that C, hitting a B♭ right before the C would not produce as much satisfaction. In other words, it wouldn't lead to the C with as much urgency. So, much like we did with the dominant chord, the B♭ would be raised to B♮ to provide that half step right before the C. But if the melody were walking up the scale for the last few notes before the final C, the note before the B would be an A♭. Moving from A♭ to B♮ produces the interval of an augmented 2nd. This interval, sounded melodically, once had an exotic character to it, especially back in 18th century Europe. And unless the piece of music was about something set in a foreign land, this exotic sound was a bit of a "no no." So, to remove this exotic sound, the A♭ was raised to A♮.

Natural Minor

Harmonic Minor

Melodic Minor

However, if a melody were not walking up to C, but descending to C, even if there were A♭s and B♭s as part of this melody, the alterations to these pitches wouldn't be needed. It is only when the melody ascends that we need the raised 6th and 7th degrees to properly lead up to the C. This is why, when we consider the melodic minor scale, we restore the 6th and 7th degrees when descending, making the melodic minor and natural minor scales the same on the way down.

SUMMARY

Scales are important in any discussion of chords and chord progressions, which will be discussed in Chapter 4. It's also important to have a basic understanding of scales and scale degree names, as these are often used in any discussion about music theory, which will also be covered in subsequent chapters in this book.

CHAPTER 3:
KEYS AND KEY SIGNATURES

At its most basic level, the circle of 5ths is a tool to help you memorize key signatures. However, an understanding of how the circle of 5ths is put together can help you figure out any key signature, should you not be able to recall it from memory.

MAJOR KEYS

At its simplest, the circle of 5ths is a graphic representation of *keys* and *key signatures*, one which demonstrates how these keys are related to one another. Consider the key of C major, which has no sharps or flats in the key signature. Using the circle of 5ths, each time we move clockwise from C, the next key has one more sharp sign in the key signature. And each new key is a 5th above the previous key on the circle. After C, G is the next key, which is a 5th up from C, and it consists of one sharp (F♯).

By the ninth position on the circle (8 o'clock, if you will), the keys change completely to those with flats. You'll also notice that there are three spots (i.e., 5, 6, and 7 o'clock) where sharp and flat keys overlap. This is for reasons of *enharmonics*, which are two notes existing as the same pitch, but spelled differently. For example, F♯ and G♭ are the same pitch (the first black key in the three-black-key set on a piano), but simply have different spellings. So, there are some key signatures which consist of the same pitches, but one is spelled with flats and the other with sharps (i.e., C♯ major and D♭ major).

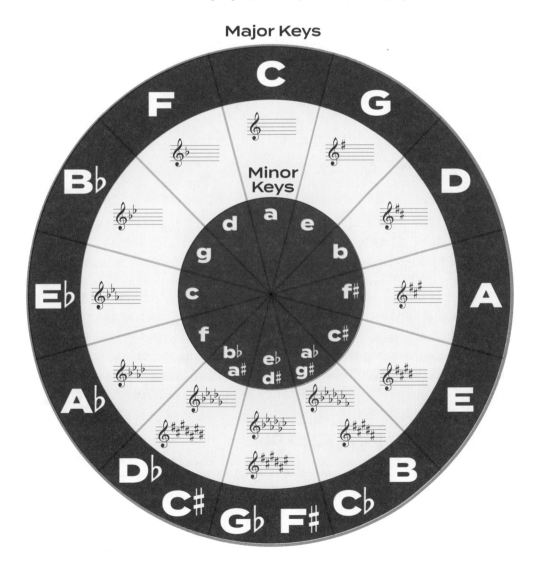

Major Keys

We've already mentioned that the inversion of the 5th is the 4th, and because of this relationship, these two intervals have similar functions to one another in music. Using the circle of 5ths, if you start on C and move counterclockwise, we start with the flat keys. Also, counterclockwise sees us moving in 4ths (i.e., F is a 4th above C, B♭ is a 4th above F, etc.).

MINOR KEYS

Every major key has a *relative minor* (and vice versa). Relative keys share the same key signature. C major and A minor are relatives of each other. On the circle of 5ths, the minor keys are illustrated in the inner circle. Logically, the minor keys are also organized in 5ths, with each new key moving clockwise on the circle being a 5th above the previous key.

So, the notes of the C major scale and the A natural minor scale are the same. The only difference is the starting pitch. But playing these pitches in this different order (i.e., "A" up to "A" compared to "C" up to "C") produces a different quality of sound, which many might say portrays a different mood, one that is darker or sadder. This is because, even though we're playing the same pitches, the half steps are in different positions, and this greatly affects the perceived mood of this sound. The same is true for how melodies and chord progressions are used.

C Major

1/2 step   1/2 step

A Minor

1/2 step   1/2 step

There is a lot which can be discussed in terms of how different keys behave, including the differences between major and minor keys (some will be covered in Chapter 4, "Chords and Progressions"). It is recommended you check out a full music theory publication for in-depth coverage on this topic.

For now, you can get a start on developing the tools needed to better learn about many music theory topics by gaining a firm grasp on key signatures. And to do this, it is highly recommended you memorize them. In doing so, be sure to not only memorize the major and minor key signatures individually, but also the pairs of relative keys. The following will cover a few methods by which you can better memorize the key signatures, while also gaining a better understanding of how they all relate to each other.

ORDER OF SHARPS

In addition to the fact that the keys are organized by 5ths, the sharps on the key signatures themselves are also organized by 5ths. For example, the key signature for D major consists of two sharps: F♯ and C♯. F is a 5th below C. Go up a 5th from C, and we arrive at G, thus the key signature with three sharps consists of F♯, C♯, and G♯. Also, these sharps always appear on the staff in that order, from left to right. Every time we add a sharp to the key signature, it is a 5th above the previous sharp.

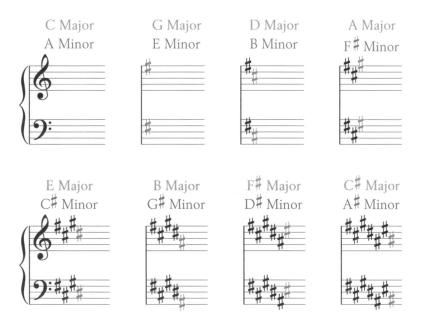

You can use the circle of 5ths to help find the order of sharps. Since we know that F# is the first sharp in the sharp key signatures, use the outer circle (major keys), start with F, and move clockwise. This will at least give you the letter names of each sharp as they appear in the key signature. For example, let's say you knew that E major consists of four sharps. To make sure you have those sharps correct and in the correct order, start with F on the circle and name the first four positions, moving clockwise: F–C–G–D.

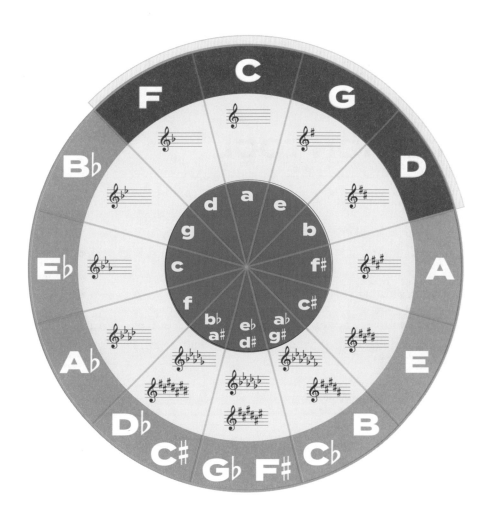

While this is one way to use the graphic image of the circle of 5ths to help name the order of sharps, it can only be handy if you really have the circle of 5ths memorized. But some find it useful to memorize the order of sharps by using a saying to go with each letter, as the following illustrates.

ORDER OF FLATS

Whereas sharps are organized in 5ths, flats are organized in 4ths. The first flat in the key signature is B♭. Move up a 4th from B♭ and we arrive on E♭. Just like moving counterclockwise on the circle of 5ths had you moving up in 4ths each time, you can use the circle of 5ths as one way to name the order of flats as they appear in the key signature. However, memorizing a saying might be even more effective for this one task, at least before you have the entire circle of 5ths memorized.

Some people use the fact that the first four flats spell the word "BEAD," then add "G–C–F" onto the end. Others come up with words for those last three letters, producing something such as "BEAD + Good Cookie Food." You can make up your own like this or invent a saying for the entire seven letters. The following is one example.

MEMORIZATION TOOL

Now that you understand how the circle of 5ths is put together, you should be able to figure out a key signature should you not have the circle of 5ths completely memorized. However, to have the circle of 5ths memorized (including being able to recall all major and minor key signatures, identify and write key signatures on the staff, and know all the pairs of relative keys) means you have a tool that can be used to engage in all types of music theory, as well as in composing, arranging, and performing. For the immediate task at hand, knowing these key signatures will allow you to better understand the discussion in the next chapter, without having to continually look back in this book.

If you're a serious student of music theory, you may wish to get yourself (or make) a circle of 5ths poster for your wall. Some people obtain circle of 5ths watches or even t-shirts. For now, make use of the following to help in your memorization objective.

Circle of 5ths Practice Tool

Use the following blank circle of 5ths diagram to practice writing the keys and key signatures. It is suggested you make copies of this diagram (before you write on it), so you can practice writing and testing yourself, repeatedly.

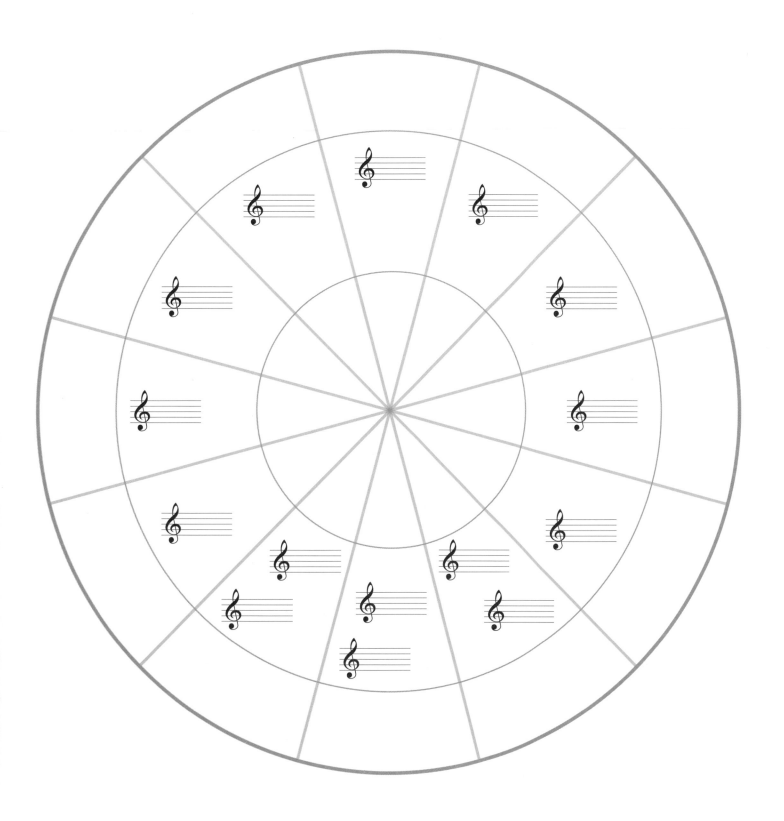

Besides filling in this blank circle of 5ths image, it is suggested you practice writing out the key signatures on the staff in both treble and bass clef. This is known as the *grand staff*, when both staves are connected together by a brace, as used in piano music. Even though you may know the order of sharps, each sharp has to be written on a specific line or space on the staff. You can't just put the sharp sign for F on any F on the staff. It must be placed (on the treble staff) on the top line. The following illustrates all key signatures, written on the grand staff.

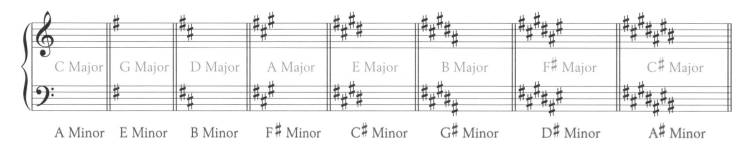

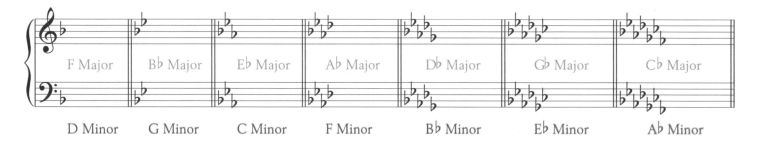

SUMMARY

Memorizing these key signatures will keep you from getting stuck or slowing you down when you attempt to examine a piece of music or begin writing a composition. Knowing these key signatures will allow you to better understand the discussion in the next chapter without the need to continually refer back in this book.

CHAPTER 4:
CHORDS AND PROGRESSIONS

Harmony is the simultaneous sounding of more than one pitch. It is often used to accompany melody. A *chord* is a type of harmony consisting of three or more pitches sounded at the same time.

TRIADS

While there are many different types of chords, in tonal music, the most frequent type is known as a *triad*. A triad is a chord consisting of three pitches, which are built in 3rds. The pitch which gives a triad its name is known as the *root*. For example, in a C major triad, C is the root. All triads consist of three parts, known as *chord tones*: a root, a 3rd, and a 5th. You might guess that these labels are based on intervals. Regardless of quality (i.e., major, minor, augmented, or diminished), all C triads consist of a C (the root), an E (the 3rd) of some kind, and a G (the 5th) of some kind.

Major Triads

All major and minor triads consist of a perfect 5th above the root. It is the quality of *3rd* which determines whether the triad is major or minor. In a *major triad*, the 3rd is major.

If you cannot immediately recall how to get to a major 3rd, one way is to remember that a major 3rd consists of four half steps. Another way to arrive at the correct spelling of a major triad is to simply use the first, third, and fifth notes of the major scale.

C Major

Eb Major

A Major

One could also use the circle of 5ths to spell major chords. For any given pitch, move clockwise around the outer circle to find the first and fourth notes. These will be the 5th and 3rd chord tones, respectively. So, including your starting pitch (the root), you'll have the three pitches for that major chord. The following illustrates this method for finding the pitches of a D major triad.

D Major Triad

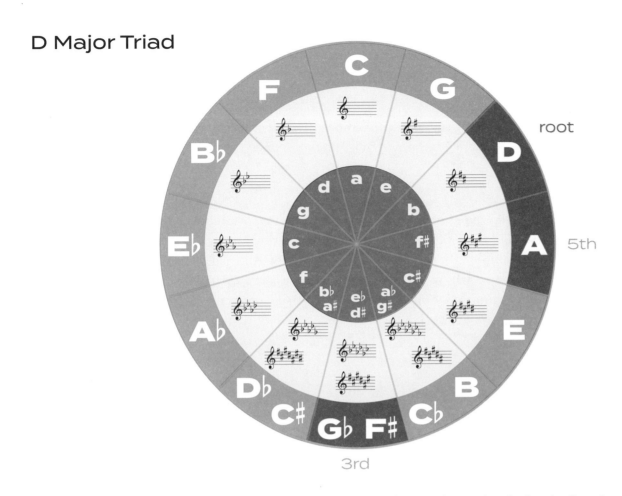

You may notice that when looking to spell the D major triad using the circle of 5ths, the fourth space clockwise held F♯ and G♭. Just remember that triads are always spelled in 3rds, so it couldn't be a G♭, since G is a 4th up from D. F♯ is a 3rd up from D.

Minor Triads

As you may have guessed, the difference between a *minor triad* and a major triad is that in the former, the 3rd above the root is minor. Similar methods which may be used to help spell major triads may be followed to spell minor triads. If you know the major triad, simply lower the 3rd a half step (retain the same letter name) and you'll have a minor triad. You may also use any of the three forms of the minor scale. Choose the 1st, 3rd, and 5th degrees of the scale to correctly spell a minor triad.

A Minor

F Minor

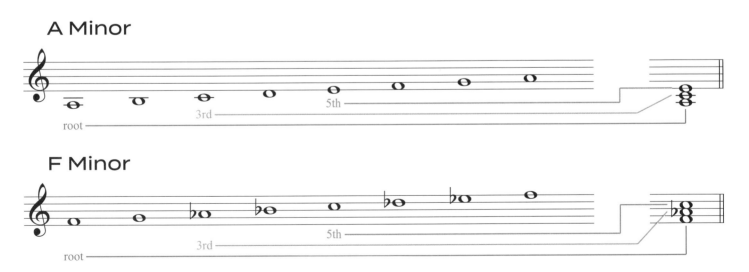

B Minor

Using the circle of 5ths from the given root, move to the first space immediately clockwise of the root to find the 5th of the chord (remember, major and minor triads both consist of the same perfect 5th up from the root). But to find the minor 3rd, move three spaces counterclockwise from the root.

C Minor Triad

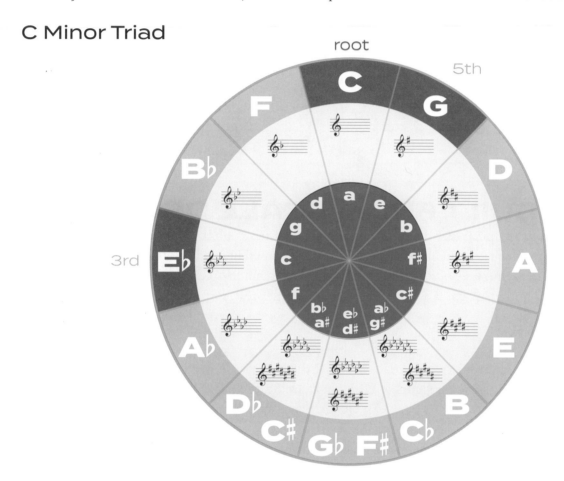

Diminished Triads

Diminished and minor triads share the same 3rd (a minor 3rd up from the root). It is the 5th that differs. In a *diminished triad*, the 5th is diminished. The easiest way to find a diminished 5th is to take a perfect 5th and shrink it by one half step (but remember to retain the same letter name). C up to G is a perfect 5th, so to find the diminished 5th up from C, lower the G to Gb, thereby shrinking the distance by one half step. And don't forget, the circle of 5ths consists of all perfect 5ths, so if you have that outer circle memorized, then you have all perfect 5ths memorized.

So, a simple way to find a diminished triad is to take the minor triad and lower the 5th one half step. (Note: the small circle "°" is the symbol used for diminished chords.)

Augmented Triads

An *augmented triad* consists of a major 3rd and an augmented 5th. Whereas taking a perfect 5th and shrinking it by one half step results in a diminished 5th, enlarging a perfect 5th by a half step gives you an augmented 5th. Similarly, taking a major triad and raising the 5th by one half step results in an augmented triad. (Note: the plus sign "+" is the symbol for "augmented.")

*The "✗" symbol above the F is a double sharp,
which raises the note by two half steps.

TRIADS BUILT FROM SCALE DEGREES

Triads can be built from any pitch of a major or minor scale. The triads built off certain scale degrees have special functions, comprising a certain hierarchy within any given key. For example, the triad built on the 1st scale degree, referred to as the *tonic triad*, is the center of gravity within that key. What that means is that the tonic triad is of central importance. It is a place where many phrases rest, sort of a "home base" of the music.

Major Scale

In major keys, the tonic triad is major. The triads built off the other scale degrees are either major, minor, or diminished. And this is the same for all major keys. For example, the chord built off the 2nd scale degree is minor. That means that whether the key is C major, A major, or D♭ major, the chord built off the 2nd scale degree is always minor. To indicate chords built off scale degrees, we use Roman numerals. This is useful when talking about keys in general, rather than discussing something within a specific key (e.g., "D major"). The following illustrates the quality of each chord built off the notes of the major scale. Note that when referring to major triads, we use uppercase Roman numerals. Augmented triads are also labeled using uppercase Roman numerals, whereas minor and diminished triads make use of lowercase numerals.

1	Tonic	Major
2	Supertonic	Minor
3	Mediant	Minor
4	Subdominant	Major
5	Dominant	Major
6	Submediant	Minor
7	Leading Tone	Diminished

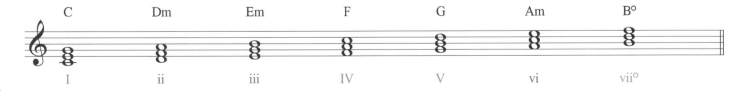

Minor Scales

Things get a little more complex when dealing with minor keys. Remember the discussion about the origin of the three different forms of the minor scale? Hopefully, that concept will start to make more sense now that we're dealing with chords. The following shows the triads built off the scale degrees of the natural minor scale.

Natural Minor

1	Tonic	Minor
2	Supertonic	Diminished
3	Mediant	Major
4	Subdominant	Minor
5	Dominant	Minor
6	Submediant	Major
7	Leading Tone	Major

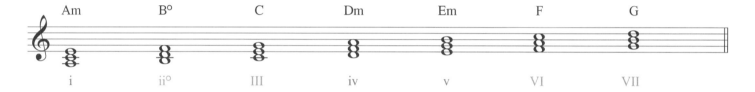

Note that the chord built from the 5th scale degree (dominant) is minor. In Chapter 2, we learned that the dominant chord is used to promote motion to the tonic chord, to produce a satisfactory punctuation or resolution at the end of a phrase. If this chord is minor, this sense of motion (the feeling, within the context of the music, that this chord wants to progress to another chord, such as the tonic chord) is absent. That is why the dominant chord is turned into a major triad, to give it this sense of motion. The following example shows each triad built off the scale degrees of the harmonic minor scale.

Harmonic Minor

1	Tonic	Minor
2	Supertonic	Diminished
3	Mediant	Augmented
4	Subdominant	Minor
5	Dominant	Major
6	Submediant	Major
7	Leading Tone	Diminished

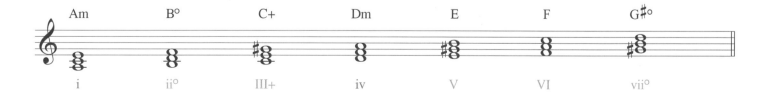

Even though the chord built on the 3rd scale degree is augmented, this is rarely used in traditional tonal music. The whole reason for the harmonic minor scale was to raise the 7th degree in order to give us the major V chord. It was not done so that we could get a distinctive augmented triad from the 3rd scale degree. However, this notion is really out of the classical music tradition, meaning today, composers are free to make use of this quirk of the harmonic minor scale as they see fit.

Melodic Minor

1	Tonic	Minor
2	Supertonic	Minor
3	Mediant	Augmented
4	Subdominant	Major
5	Dominant	Major
6	Submediant	Diminished
7	Leading Tone	Diminished

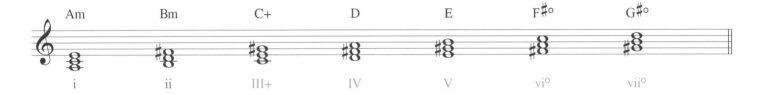

Notice that because of the raised 7th degree, the chord built off that note of the scale ends up being the same as in the *parallel* major key ("parallel" refers to two keys with the same tonic, such as C major and C minor). In other words, in both A major and A minor, the vii° is diminished. This is done for a particular function. The interval between the root and 5th is a diminished 5th, otherwise known as a *tritone*. It is a particularly dissonant interval, meaning it sounds tense, like it wants to resolve to something more stable. As a result, the vii° chord is often used to produce a particularly strong pull back to the tonic chord. In the following example, the tritone exists between G♯ and D. This resolves inward (the G♯ resolves up to A and the D resolves down to C/C♯).

The melodic minor scale was created to avoid the uncharacteristic leap of the augmented 2nd in a melody. As such, it was not done to give us a variety of different chords compared to those built from the notes of the natural minor scale. However, as was mentioned in the previous discussion of the harmonic minor scale, composers may wish to make use of these chords for greater harmonic flavor.

7TH CHORDS

Where triads consist of three chord tones, *7th chords* consist of four: a root, 3rd, 5th, and 7th, with the latter being a 7th above the root.

The following are the most commonly used types of 7th chords, although there are more. The type or quality of a 7th chord is determined by the quality of triad plus the quality of the 7th.

CHORD NAME	TRIAD	7TH
Dominant 7th	major	minor
Minor 7th	minor	minor
Major 7th	major	major
Fully Diminished 7th	diminished	diminished
Half Diminished 7th (sometimes labeled "m7♭5" in popular music notation)	diminished	minor

While there are several different types or qualities of 7th chords, arguably the most important is the *dominant 7th chord*. This chord consists of a major triad plus a minor 7th. It is called a "dominant 7th chord" because if you construct 7th chords from each scale degree, the only place where this type of chord occurs is built from the 5th degree. In modern music notation, the chord symbol for the dominant 7th chord consists simply of the letter plus the number seven. The following shows the variety of 7th chords built from each degree of the major scale.

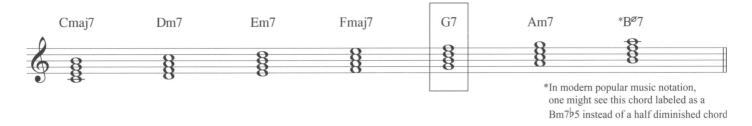

*In modern popular music notation, one might see this chord labeled as a Bm7♭5 instead of a half diminished chord

In minor keys, we usually see the 7th chord built from the 5th scale degree in the form of the dominant 7th chord. In other words, the triad is turned into a major chord in raising the 7th degree of the scale for the same reasons previously covered. The following example shows the most common 7th chords in a minor key. (Note: the scale doesn't strictly follow either the natural minor or the harmonic minor, rather the raised 7th degree of the scale, G♯ in this case, is used here to produce the major triad in the dominant 7th chord as well as the diminished chord built from the 7th scale degree).

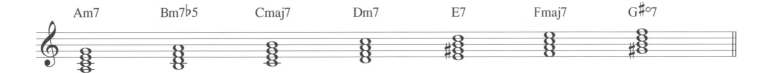

While in traditional rock and pop music, the 7th chord is largely saved for the dominant, in jazz, and other adventurous styles of music, 7ths are often added to chords built off all scale degrees to produce extra harmonic flavor. But it's not only 7ths that are added. If you keep stacking more 3rds onto the top of a chord, you get 9th, 11th, and 13th chords. There is not a 15th chord, because the tone that's a 15th above the root is the same pitch as the root.

CHORD PROGRESSIONS

We've already discussed how the dominant chord is important in that it is used to lead back to the tonic chord, especially at the ends of phrases. The instability of the dominant chord, and thus its "want" to resolve to the tonic, is made even stronger when we add the minor 7th above the root. This is due to the tritone interval, which occurs between the 7th and the 3rd of the chord.

The concept of *progression* is governed in part by this "want," the tendency of the dominant chord to resolve to the tonic. The tritone in the dominant 7th chord tends to resolve inwards to a 3rd. In this case, the tritone between B and F resolves inward to C and E, which are the root and 3rd of the tonic chord (C).

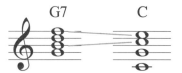

Some chords feel stable within the context of any given phrase, while others feel unstable (or less stable). Instability promotes motion, and motion from one chord to the next is governed by the tension and release created by instability and stability. It is this motion that makes for *true* chord progressions, rather than simply a series of chords, one after another.

Since the subject of chord progressions could make for a large book on its own, this discussion will focus on progressions which see the interval of the 5th/4th functioning as a major factor.

Primary Chords

There are endless possibilities of chord progressions, even among those that are quite simple. At the heart of a lot of popular and even classical music are progressions which involve only three chords within a given key. These three chords are built off the 1st, 4th, and 5th scale degrees, known as *primary chords*.

Whereas the dominant chord is a 5th above the tonic, the subdominant chord is a 5th below. This is another way the interval of the 5th/4th shows itself to be at the heart of tonal music. You can use the circle of 5ths to find the primary chords of any key, very easily. Simply locate the name of your key in the outer circle, and then the two spaces on either side of the key comprise the primary chords. The IV chord is immediately counterclockwise from the tonic, while the V chord is the first space clockwise. The following example illustrates the key of D major.

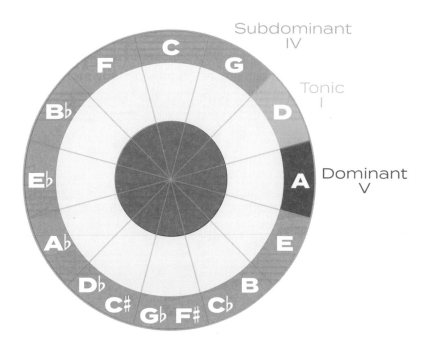

Countless rock 'n' roll and blues tunes make use of the primary chords, and only the primary chords. There are quite a few classical pieces which follow this simple harmonic design, as well. With both chords having a 4th/5th relationship to the tonic, the tension and release between each chord and the tonic has a kind of tonic/dominant relationship.

Chords next to each other on the circle of 5ths will seem to have tonic/dominant relationships, promoting a satisfying series of tension and release moments. The following is a simple rock/blues progression, making use of the primary chords.

Circle Progressions

Circle progressions include chords related by 5ths/4ths. Chords with roots are next to each other on the circle of 5ths comprise progressions which provide a certain amount of satisfying harmonic motion. The next few examples will expand upon the simple blues-like progression by adding additional chords related by 5ths/4ths. These progressions are also *diatonic*, meaning, they don't involve adding accidentals to provide any pitches outside of the key.

The first makes use of the primary chords in the key of C (C, F, and G), plus the ii chord, which is one space clockwise from the G chord. In the key of C, the ii is a D minor triad.

This progression, which occurs twice over the last six bars, is often referred to as the "ii–V–I" progression. It should be noted that, except for the V7 chord (G7), this blues progression uses only triads, rather than 7th chords. The use of 7th chords based on all scale degrees is more common in order to give a blues-based tune its distinctive flavor.

We could use the same type of blues music to demonstrate one step further, adding an A chord, which would result from the inclusion of one more space clockwise on the circle. However, let's advance things a bit more and add two more spaces on the circle, giving us A and E chords. In C major, both of these chords would be minor. The full progression now includes six consecutive spaces on the outer circle, giving us the following chords.

I	C
IV	F
V7	G7
ii	Dm
vi	Am
iii	Em

But in order to make this a true circle progression, the order in which these chords appear is important. While the F (IV) chord—the only chord countercloc kwise from the tonic—is sounded frequently near the beginning of the excerpt, it is towards the latter part of the excerpt (measures 8–11) where we see the chords appearing consecutively, one space on the circle to the next.

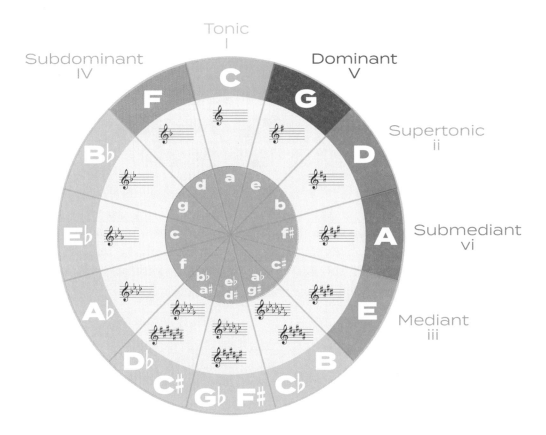

You might have noticed that, in terms of chords built off pitches of the major scale, we are missing one: the leading-tone chord. In the key of C major, this would be a B° triad. While we could throw this chord into the mix, placing it right before the Em (iii) chord in some way, using the vii° chord in this way is a bit less traditional. Plus, it really starts to turn this whole circle progression concept into too much of a formula, which could come off sounding mechanical and stilted. However, there are creative ways it could be achieved.

The previous examples made use of a standard blues progression, one that is also common in a lot of rock and pop music. In addition, circle progressions are prevalent in classical music, with many of the great composers making use of this harmonic concept.

Let's try this in a minor key. The following is set in C minor, and unlike the previous example where the circle progression took place near the end of the excerpt, this illustrates a case where an entire section, such as a verse or chorus of a song, can be made up of one complete circle progression. Note that this makes use of all diatonic chords (chords based on each pitch of the C minor scale).

The following illustrates the names of each chord root on the circle of 5ths. Since this excerpt is in a minor key you could use the inner circle, but that is not necessary. Since we are not dealing with keys, rather just the names of chords, you could use either the inner circle or the outer. Both are arranged in 5ths, and both display the same order. Just keep in mind that the circle of 5ths does not show chord quality, only the letter names of each chord root. It should be noted that while the circle progression moves from one space to the next (counterclockwise), because the distance from the VI chord to the ii° (A♭ to D°) is a tritone, we must jump across to the opposite side of the circle at that point. So, whether you use the inner circle or the outer, begin with C and move counterclockwise, and all chords will match the excerpt.

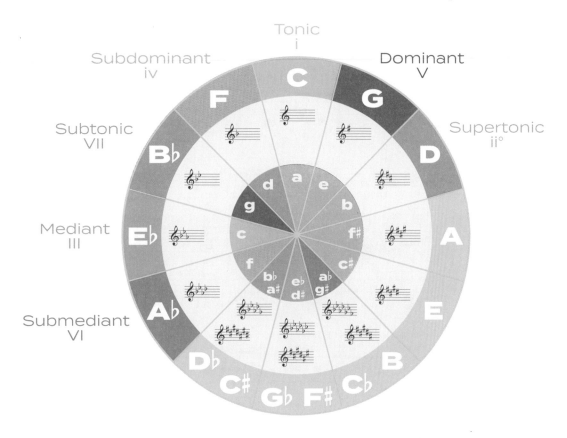

MODULATION

Modulation is a process by which a piece of music changes key. In other words, a new pitch and thus a new chord becomes the tonic. A piece of music cannot simply land on a new chord and sit on it for a while in order for this process to take hold. There needs to be a way of establishing that a new tonic is "in charge." One of the most traditional ways to do this is to precede the new tonic with its respective dominant 7th chord, and to do so at the end and/or beginning of a phrase. This is yet another way in which the interval of the 5th has great strength and power in its ability to initiate substantial change within a piece of music.

While the previous circle progression examples stuck with diatonic chords, many examples exist in which certain pitches have been chromatically altered to produce different quality chords. In our example, rather than sound a Dm chord (naturally occurring in the key of C major), this harmony could be turned into a D major chord by raising the F to F♯. Given that a D major triad is the true dominant of G, sounding it in the key of C produces the effect of instability. The ear expects the D chord to be followed by G (G major or G minor), and if a G chord does indeed follow the D, it sounds welcome and satisfying. If we were to take the D chord and add the minor 7th (C), we'd get a complete V7 chord (of G). That tritone between the F♯ and C increases the instability, letting the listener really know that change is afoot. The following example gives us the D7 chord in measure 7, which eventually resolves to the G chord in measure 9.

Any chord that is altered through the use of accidentals, turning it into a dominant 7th chord, is known as a *secondary dominant*. It is secondary in that it is not the dominant of the tonic chord, rather it is dominant of another chord. Note that the D7 in measure 7 is preceded by an Am chord, which is related by a 5th to D. This makes for a circle progression, moving from Am to D7 to G, while also allowing for the modulation to the key of G major. The Am chord is also a harmony which occurs naturally in both the keys of C major and G major. This is known as a *pivot chord*, something which can help a modulation seem smooth.

Also note that in measures 9–11, we see a back and forth between the G and D7 chord. This helps firmly establish the new key by reinforcing the new tonic/dominant relationship between G and D. Sometimes, a secondary dominant chord sets up a new key, but the key change is only temporary. If our example hadn't reinforced the new key of G major in measures 9–11 (especially measures 10–11), but returned to C major, then this might not be a true key change, rather a *tonicization* of G. Secondary dominants are sometimes used to give extra weight to a chord other than the tonic, for a variety of reasons. Think of it as if the tonic were the captain of a ship. If the captain were to be out of commission for a bit, all the captain's authority might rest in the hands of the first officer, briefly. This doesn't mean we have a new captain, only that the first officer has the same responsibilities, temporarily.

The previous example saw a modulation between two "closely related keys" (there is only one pitch different between C major and G major: the F♯). When modulating between two keys which are more distantly related, the circle of 5ths can be used to help the transition remain smooth. Taking the same basic music as in the previous example, the next couple excerpts will see the music changing key from C major to A♭ major, but in two different ways. The first method travels through a circle progression until reaching an E♭ chord, then adds the 7th to make this an E♭7 chord, which is the dominant of A♭.

Beginning in measure 4, the harmony follows a strict circle progression. Notice how the music keeps changing key as it moves through the circle progression as opposed to earlier, when we used only diatonic chords in the key of C. With this method, turning every chord into a dominant 7th gives the impression of constantly changing key, albeit briefly, instead of just moving through a series of different chords within one key.

The second method of modulating to a more distantly related key is more direct, but less smooth. Just how jarring the effect is happens to be in the eye of the beholder. If you're a composer, this may be exactly the type of effect you're seeking. With this method, given the target key (A♭ major, in this case), simply determine the dominant of that key (a 5th above the given pitch), sound that chord, and then make it a dominant 7th to create the demand that it resolve to its respective tonic. From the previous example, we already know that E♭ is the dominant of A♭.

Moving abruptly to the E♭ chord, without traveling in the smoother sounding circle, can be described as moving to the E♭ chord *without preparation*. To *prepare* for a certain chord, especially one that is *chromatic* (outside of the given key), means to precede it with its respective dominant. (Note that besides preceding a chord with its respective dominant, the leading-tone chord is another way to prepare. Remember, a leading tone chord is a diminished chord a half step below the target chord.)

Whether you travel in a circle involving several chords, or move quickly as in the last example, both methods involve the tonic/dominant relationship to establish the new key. In other words, the interval of the 5th/4th is important in fully establishing a new key, no matter how quickly you get there.

SUMMARY

Whether dealing with keys and key signatures, scales, chords and chord progressions, or trying to memorize intervals, the circle of 5ths can be an important tool in helping you achieve your goals. It also demonstrates very effectively how different musical concepts and structural elements are all connected. While there may be faster or easier ways to find certain answers when studying music theory, having the circle of 5ths fully memorized can at the very least serve as a backup. And understanding how the circle is organized means you always have a way to double-check your work, ensuring you're able to proceed in your endeavors with confidence.

Great Harmony & Theory Helpers

HAL LEONARD HARMONY & THEORY
by George Heussenstamm
Hal Leonard

These books are designed for anyone wishing to expand their knowledge of music theory, whether beginner or more advanced. The first two chapters deal with music fundamentals, and may be skipped by those with music reading experience.

00312062 Part 1 – Diatonic $27.50
00312064 Part 2 – Chromatic $27.50

BERKLEE MUSIC THEORY BOOK 1 – 2ND EDITION
by Paul Schmeling
Berklee Press

This essential method features rigorous, hands-on, "ears-on" practice exercises that help you explore the inner working of music, presenting notes, scales, and rhythms as they are heard in pop, jazz, and blues. You will learn and build upon the basic concepts of music theory with written exercises, listening examples, and ear training exercises.

50449615 .... $24.99

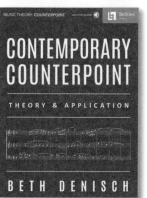

CONTEMPORARY COUNTERPOINT
Theory & Application
by Beth Denisch
Berklee Press

Use counterpoint to make your music more engaging and creative. Counterpoint – the relationship between musical voices – is among the core principles for writing music, and it has been central to the study of composition for many centuries. Whether you are a composer, arranger, film composer, orchestrator, music director, bandleader, or improvising musician, this book will help hone your craft, gain control, and lead you to new creative possibilities.

00147050 .... $22.99

THE CHORD WHEEL
The Ultimate Tool for All Musicians
by Jim Fleser
Hal Leonard

Master chord theory ... in minutes! *The Chord Wheel* is a revolutionary device that puts the most essential and practical applications of chord theory into your hands. This tool will help you: Improvise and Solo – Talk about chops! Comprehend key structure like never before; Transpose Keys – Instantly transpose any progression into each and every key; Compose Your Own Music – Watch your songwriting blossom! No music reading is necessary.

00695579 .... $15.99

ENCYCLOPEDIA OF READING RHYTHMS
Text and Workbook for All Instruments
by Gary Hess
Musicians Institute Press

A comprehensive guide to notes, rests, counting, subdividing, time signatures, triplets, ties, dotted notes and rests, cut time, compound time, swing, shuffle, rhythm studies, counting systems, road maps and more!

00695145 .... $29.99

HARMONY AND THEORY
A Comprehensive Source for All Musicians
by Keith Wyatt and Carl Schroeder
Musicians Institute Press

This book is a step-by-step guide to MI's well-known Harmony and Theory class. It includes complete lessons and analysis of: intervals, rhythms, scales, chords, key signatures; transposition, chord inversions, key centers; harmonizing the major and minor scales; and more!

00695161 .... $22.99

MUSIC THEORY WORKBOOK
For All Musicians
by Chris Bowman
Hal Leonard

A self-study course with illustrations and examples for you to write and check your answers. Topics include: major and minor scales; modes and other scales; harmony; intervals; chord structure; chord progressions and substitutions; and more.

00101379 .... $12.99

JAZZOLOGY
The Encyclopedia of Jazz Theory for All Musicians
by Robert Rawlins and Nor Eddine Bahha
Hal Leonard

A one-of-a-kind book encompassing a wide scope of jazz topics, for beginners and pros of any instrument. A three-pronged approach was envisioned with the creation of this comprehensive resource: as an encyclopedia for ready reference, as a thorough methodology for the student, and as a workbook for the classroom, complete with ample exercises and conceptual discussion.

00311167 .... $19.99

Jazz Instruction & Improvisation

BOOKS FOR ALL INSTRUMENTS FROM HAL LEONARD

AN APPROACH TO JAZZ IMPROVISATION
by Dave Pozzi
Musicians Institute Press
Explore the styles of Charlie Parker, Sonny Rollins, Bud Powell and others with this comprehensive guide to jazz improvisation. Covers: scale choices • chord analysis • phrasing • melodies • harmonic progressions • more.
00695135 Book/CD Pack.........................$17.95

THE ART OF MODULATING
FOR PIANISTS AND JAZZ MUSICIANS
by Carlos Salzedo &
Lucile Lawrence
Schirmer
The Art of Modulating is a treatise originally intended for the harp, but this edition has been edited for use by intermediate keyboardists and other musicians who have an understanding of basic music theory. In its pages you will find: table of intervals; modulation rules; modulation formulas; examples of modulation; extensions and cadences; ten fragments of dances; five characteristic pieces; and more.
50490581 ....$19.99

BUILDING A JAZZ VOCABULARY
By Mike Steinel
A valuable resource for learning the basics of jazz from Mike Steinel of the University of North Texas. It covers: the basics of jazz • how to build effective solos • a comprehensive practice routine • and a jazz vocabulary of the masters.
00849911 ....$19.99

THE CYCLE OF FIFTHS
by Emile and Laura De Cosmo
This essential instruction book provides more than 450 exercises, including hundreds of melodic and rhythmic ideas. The book is designed to help improvisors master the cycle of fifths, one of the primary progressions in music. Guaranteed to refine technique, enhance improvisational fluency, and improve sight-reading!
00311114 ....$16.99

THE DIATONIC CYCLE
by Emile and Laura De Cosmo
Renowned jazz educators Emile and Laura De Cosmo provide more than 300 exercises to help improvisors tackle one of music's most common progressions: the diatonic cycle. This book is guaranteed to refine technique, enhance improvisational fluency, and improve sight-reading!
00311115 ....$16.95

EAR TRAINING
by Keith Wyatt,
Carl Schroeder and Joe Elliott
Musicians Institute Press
Covers: basic pitch matching • singing major and minor scales • identifying intervals • transcribing melodies and rhythm • identifying chords and progressions • seventh chords and the blues • modal interchange, chromaticism, modulation • and more.
00695198 Book/Online Audio $24.99

EXERCISES AND ETUDES FOR THE JAZZ INSTRUMENTALIST
by J.J. Johnson
Designed as study material and playable by any instrument, these pieces run the gamut of the jazz experience, featuring common and uncommon time signatures and keys, and styles from ballads to funk. They are progressively graded so that both beginners and professionals will be challenged by the demands of this wonderful music.
00842018 Bass Clef Edition $19.99
00842042 Treble Clef Edition $16.95

JAZZOLOGY
THE ENCYCLOPEDIA OF JAZZ THEORY FOR ALL MUSICIANS
by Robert Rawlins and
Nor Eddine Bahha
This comprehensive resource covers a variety of jazz topics, for beginners and pros of any instrument. The book serves as an encyclopedia for reference, a thorough methodology for the student, and a workbook for the classroom.
00311167 ....$19.99

JAZZ THEORY RESOURCES
by Bert Ligon
Houston Publishing, Inc.
This is a jazz theory text in two volumes. **Volume 1 includes**: review of basic theory • rhythm in jazz performance • triadic generalization • diatonic harmonic progressions and analysis • substitutions and turnarounds • and more. **Volume 2 includes**: modes and modal frameworks • quartal harmony • extended tertian structures and triadic superimposition • pentatonic applications • coloring "outside" the lines and beyond • and more.
00030458 Volume 1 ....$39.99
00030459 Volume 2 ....$32.99

HAL•LEONARD®
7777 W. BLUEMOUND RD. P.O. BOX 13819 MILWAUKEE, WI 53213

Visit Hal Leonard online at
www.halleonard.com

JOY OF IMPROV
by Dave Frank
and John Amaral
This book/audio course on improvisation for all instruments and all styles will help players develop monster musical skills! **Book One** imparts a solid basis in technique, rhythm, chord theory, ear training and improv concepts. **Book Two** explores more advanced chord voicings, chord arranging techniques and more challenging blues and melodic lines. The audio can be used as a listening and play-along tool.
00220005 Book 1 – Book/Online Audio...............$27.99
00220006 Book 2 – Book/Online Audio...............$26.99

THE PATH TO JAZZ IMPROVISATION
by Emile and Laura De Cosmo
This fascinating jazz instruction book offers an innovative, scholarly approach to the art of improvisation. It includes in-depth analysis and lessons about: cycle of fifths • diatonic cycle • overtone series • pentatonic scale • harmonic and melodic minor scale • polytonal order of keys • blues and bebop scales • modes • and more.
00310904 ....$19.99

THE SOURCE
THE DICTIONARY OF CONTEMPORARY AND TRADITIONAL SCALES
by Steve Barta
This book serves as an informative guide for people who are looking for good, solid information regarding scales, chords, and how they work together. It provides right and left hand fingerings for scales, chords, and complete inversions. Includes over 20 different scales, each written in all 12 keys.
00240885 ....$19.99

21 BEBOP EXERCISES
by Steve Rawlins
This book/CD pack is both a warm-up collection and a manual for bebop phrasing. Its tasty and sophisticated exercises will help you develop your proficiency with jazz interpretation. It concentrates on practice in all twelve keys – moving higher by half-step – to help develop dexterity and range. The companion CD includes all of the exercises in 12 keys.
00315341 Book/CD Pack...................................$17.95

Prices, contents & availability
subject to change without notice.